C000112131

BRANDING YOURSELF:

10 STEPS TOWARDS TURNING YOUR PASSION INTO BRAND IDENTITY

KAIROS
ONLINE
MARKETING

TABLE OF CONTENTS:

KAIROS
ONLINE
MARKETING

Introduction:

Have you ever wondered why certain individuals in your field rise out of nowhere to national prominence? These experts get all the media attention, deliver keynotes at top conferences and attract the best clients. Are these men and women just smarter than the rest of us? Or are they privy to some magical personal branding strategy that the rest of us don't know about?

Instead, they developed their personal branding strategies the hard way, through trial and error. That means each one of them followed a different path, trying and discarding a host of tools and techniques along the way.

Apple challenged the world to "Think Different." Nike encouraged people, regardless of age, gender, or physical fitness level, to "Just Do It." Dunkin' Donuts persuaded busy professionals that "America Runs on Dunkin'."

Over the years, these recognizable slogans have morphed into rallying cries—setting the tone for how each company communicates and identifies itself in the market. In just a handful of words, these slogans have told a story and influenced how people perceive the organizations behind them. Together, they represent the power and potential of branding.

"Branding is what companies stand for," says Dr. Sean Gresh, a faculty member in Northeastern's Master of Science in Corporate and Organizational Communication program. "It's reflected in how that company acts, how it serves people, the value that the company shares, and how the company projects those values."

A strong brand stands out in the crowd—and gains more sales, increased awareness, and better customer experiences as a result.

But branding isn't just for companies. Professionals each have their own story to tell and goals, skills, and expertise to share. In today's increasingly digital world, a personal brand is no longer a nice-to-have; it's expected.

Now, the last thing I want to do is discourage you. Building a successful personal brand — one that propels you to prominence in your field — is actually easier than it looks.

Remember, from the bottom of the mountain the summit always looks unattainable. But if you focus on the process of getting there — taking one small step at a time — you'll find yourself looking down with amazement at the world you left behind. It's a journey well worth taking!

What Is A Personal Brand Strategy?

Let's start with the basics. A personal branding strategy is a plan to take your reputation and career from relative obscurity to high visibility. It describes where you stand today and what level of visibility you want to achieve in the future. Then it lays out in detail the tactics, tools and skills you will need to attain your goal, including the daily content calendar that will guide your daily journey. A carefully planned strategy takes the uncertainty out of your quest for Visible Expertise so that you can concentrate on carrying it out.

A modern personal branding strategy is strongly rooted in content marketing.

What Is A Personal Brand?

A personal brand is, in many ways, similar to a corporate brand, Gresh explains. It is who you are, what you stand for, the values you embrace, and the way in which you express those values. Just as a company's brand helps to communicate its value to customers and stand out from the competition, a personal brand does the same for individuals, helping to communicate a unique identity and clear value to potential employers or clients.

Or, as Gresh summarizes: "Personal branding is one's story."

That story can play an important role in establishing or boosting your career. In fact, an overwhelming 85 percent of hiring managers report that a job candidate's personal brand influences their hiring decisions. Your personal brand should highlight your strengths, establish a reputation, build trust, and communicate the unique attributes that you bring to your current (or desired) industry. Cultivated well, your personal brand will signal to employers whether or not you'll be the right fit for an open role.

10 Tips For Building Your Personal Brand:

Developing a personal brand might sound challenging, but there are incremental steps you can take to build credibility in your field. Here are ten tips to help you create an authentic personal brand—and amplify your career in the process.

1. Figure Out Who You Are:

In order to build a personal brand that accurately reflects your personal and professional identity, you first need to know who you are. Be introspective, and create a list of your personal strengths and weaknesses.

Ask yourself:

In which areas of work do I excel?

What motivates me?

What characteristics have others complimented me on?

Which projects have others had to help me with repeatedly?

Which roles seem to drain my energy?

Which projects can I spend hours on without feeling overwhelmed or tired?

If you're struggling to answer these questions, ask friends, family, and co-workers how they would describe you. Once you're more aware of the different facets of your personality, you can decide how best to brand them.

Keep in mind that many people struggle to choose a specific niche because they don't want to limit themselves. Realize that your personal brand, like many corporate brands, will change as your career grows. The best strategy is to choose a particular area you'd like to focus on and let it evolve over time.

2. Choose What You Will Be Known For:

Your personal brand is more than a reflection of who you are today; it's a roadmap of where you to go. In addition to understanding your existing skills and competencies, Gresh suggests assessing your strengths and weaknesses as they relate to whichever industry or career you want to break into next.

By doing this, you'll uncover the skills and traits that make you distinct, as well as the areas where you need to improve or gain new knowledge in order to advance.

Forecasting where you want to be in five or 10 years— and the attributes you want to be known for—can help you better determine what steps you need to take in order to get there.

3. Define Your

Audience:

Before you start crafting your personal brand, you also need to determine who you're trying to reach. Is it other industry thought leaders? An individual at a particular company? Recruiters? The sooner you define the audience, the easier it will be to craft your story, because you'll better understand the type of story you need to tell (and where you need to tell it.)

For example, if your goal is to reach hiring managers and recruiters, you might start by creating or updating your LinkedIn profile. Why? Because 92 percent of recruiters leverage social media to find high-quality candidates and, of those, 87 percent use LinkedIn.

On the other hand, if you are a graphic designer trying to impress existing clientele and attract new customers, you might choose to tell your story via a personal website or portfolio, where you can better express your wide range of talents.

4. Research Your Desired Industry And Follow The Experts:

As you start mapping out the careers you want, Gresh recommends compiling research on experts in those roles.

"Find out who the thought leaders are in whatever field you're interested in, and don't just follow them," he says.

"Go online and find out if they have blogs, or where they contribute their thinking. Look for people who are successful and examine what they're doing. Imitate them, and then do one better."

In building a personal brand, your goal is to stand out— but you can't rise to the top without taking inventory of who's already there.

5. Ask For Informational Interviews:

As you start forming a list of companies you aspire to work for and industry leaders you admire, consider reaching out to these professionals to ask for an informational interview.

"They take 20 minutes, but are of high value," Gresh says. "Don't be afraid to ask anyone you're interested in learning more from. You'd be surprised by how genuine and generous people are."

When you meet with these individuals, ask questions that can help you garner new insights about your desired field, such as:

How did you break into the industry?

What steps would you take if you were to make the transition all over again?

How do you see the industry evolving?

How do you stay up-to-date with industry trends?

Are there any professional or trade associations I should join?

According to Gresh, informational interviews come with an added benefit: "You're learning about what it takes to get into the profession, but you're also sharing in the course of this dialogue a little bit about yourself. What you're doing is building your brand."

Although there might not be a job on the line in one of these interviews, one day there could be—and you want that employer to think of you when he or she is envisioning the ideal candidate.

6. Prepare An Elevator Pitch:

As you begin to conceptualize your personal brand, spend some time crafting an elevator pitch—a 30- to 60-second story about who you are. Whether you're attending a networking event or an informal party, having an elevator pitch prepared makes it easy to describe succinctly what you do and where you're going (or would like to go) in your career.

"You need to come up with very short, concise things to say—stories to tell—that frame your attributes in the right light," says Frank Cutitta, founder of the Center for Global Branding and a Northeastern University graduate professor who teaches a course on personal branding.

Keep your elevator pitch brief by focusing on a few key points you want to emphasize. This could include that you're looking for a new position, have strengths in a particular niche, or recently increased the value of your current department or company.

7. Embrace

Networking:

As you cultivate your ideal personal brand, it's important to network regularly (and effectively) to grow your professional circle. Connect with peers and industry thought-leaders by going to formal and informal networking events.

The more connections you make—and the more value you can provide in your interactions—the more likely it is your personal brand will be recognized. And, considering 85 percent of all jobs are filled through networking, regularly attending these events will help you not only build your brand, but potentially advance your career, too.

At these events, don't be shy about asking fellow attendees to meet again for an informational interview or a casual coffee chat. And remember, if you don't get a chance to connect at the event, reach out via email or LinkedIn to spark a conversation.

8. Ask For

Recommendations:

Having current and former colleagues and managers

endorse you is one of the easiest and most effective

ways to define your personal brand, allowing others to

communicate your value for you. Just as a business

might cultivate customer reviews and testimonials for

use in sales and marketing collateral, you too should

cultivate your own reviews in the form of

recommendations.

LinkedIn is a great place to ask for endorsements because these recommendations will likely catch the eye of future hiring managers. But don't forget to ask the people endorsing you to act as an actual reference during your job search, being sure they're willing to speak with a potential employer or write a bonafide letter of recommendation if needed.

Not sure who to ask? Former managers who mentored you closely are ideal, but other connections can also craft effective recommendations, including professors and leaders of organizations you belong to.

9. Grow Your Online

Presence:

One of the most important aspects of personal branding is making sure your online presence is engaging to hiring managers, co-workers, and others— even if you're not on the job hunt.

With so many different social media tools available today, your online presence will likely look different depending on the medium you choose. While your story should match across all platforms, once you know where your targeted audience is most likely to turn, you can redouble your efforts in telling your best story there.

Additionally, if you want one of your sites or profiles to be exclusively for friends and family, adjust your privacy settings to ensure that potential employers don't stumble upon any information that could potentially harm your chances of landing a job. Here are some platform-specific tips to help you effectively craft your personal brand online.

A. LinkedIn

LinkedIn serves as a professional social media tool and is the ultimate site for defining your brand. The best way to use this network is to participate in groups, make introductions with people who interest you, and ask for (and give) recommendations. Some other tips for effectively telling your story through LinkedIn include:

I. Focus On Key Industry Skills

II. Quantify Your Accomplishments

III. Complete Your Profile

IV. Use A professional Photo

<u>I. Focus On Key</u>

<u>Industry Skills:</u>

Recruiters will often search for keywords that relate to the role they're trying to fill, so it's important to feature industry terms in your profile—whether in your headline, summary, or job description—and explicitly state your skills. For example, if you're pursuing a communications role, zero in on your area of interest and key qualifications, such as public relations, social media, or crisis communication.

II. Quantify Your Accomplishments:

Saying you're "results-oriented" isn't nearly as effective as your actual results. Quantify your accomplishments when possible, whether it's the number of articles you've written, dollars you've raised, or deals you've closed.

III. Complete Your

Profile:

While this might sound obvious, it's not uncommon for users to leave sections of their LinkedIn profile blank. Recruiters want to see what work experience you have, your educational background, and a detailed list of accomplishments, so make sure you're showing the full picture. Convince them you're the person they should hire.

IV. Use A Professional

Photo:

LinkedIn users with a professional headshot receive 14 times more profile views than those without. Upload a current photo that's closely cropped to your face. Remember, you should be the focal point, so avoid any busy backgrounds—and smile. The more welcoming you look, the more likely recruiters are to contact you

B. Twitter

Leverage this platform to highlight and build upon your industry expertise. Try to incorporate your personal brand into your Twitter bio by using hashtags to focus on your niche, following leaders in your field, and retweeting top industry stories. Don't forget: what you tweet is still a part of your online image.

C. Personal Website Or Portfolio

If you're in a marketing or design field, it's especially important to have a personal website or portfolio that provides essential information about who you are and helps visually highlight your work. You can create your own site using Squarespace, Wix, or WordPress, among others. Small brands and business owners can also take advantage of helpful design resources like Canva and Venngage's logo templates to get started creating brand-specific content.

10. Remember That Your Personal Brand Isn't Just Online:

Your brand is more than just an online persona; it's how you carry yourself at home, in the office, and even on your daily commute.

"Your reputation is everything," Gresh emphasizes. "Those who frustrate or annoy others—that will come back to haunt them. The more opportunities you have to work with others, volunteer for projects, and assert yourself as a leader, take them. That's part of your brand."

Leadership isn't reserved for C-suite executives. Strong leaders exist at every level of the organization. "Leadership comes from how you behave, how you act, and how you inherently interact with people," Gresh says. "That's real leadership."

That story you tell, combined with those everyday interactions, ultimately define your personal brand.

Reinvent Your Personal Brand As You Grow!

As the digital ecosystem changes and your career evolves, so will your personal brand. Adjust your persona accordingly as you meet different people, find new networking opportunities, and grow in your career. As long as it reflects your professional life, don't hesitate to create a brand that lets you shine.

BRANDING YOURSELF:

10 STEPS TOWARDS TURNING YOUR PASSION INTO BRAND IDENTITY

KAIROS
ONLINE
MARKETING

Printed in Great Britain
by Amazon

15708630R00025